Understanding Intelligence

THE SIMPLE TRUTH BEHIND THE
BRAIN'S ULTIMATE SECRET

Rocco Van Schalkwyk

ISBN 979-8-5158-9647-8

DISCLAIMER

The explanation of intelligence in this book offers a way to define intelligence in a simple and understandable manner. It is not based on an in-depth analysis or understanding of the neurophysiology of the brain or on an extensive knowledge of psychological principles. It is a 'functional' approach that can easily be translated into mathematical terms and coded into computer programs for robotic applications.

CONTENTS

WHAT WILL YOU LEARN IN THIS BOOK?

Introduction

Welcome to this journey of discovery into the human mind where I will reveal to you the simple secrets around how intelligence works in the brain.

The simple 'easy-to-read' approach presented here will help you avoid the many different, often complex and conflicting views that neurologists, psychologists and philosophers hold as to what intelligence is and how it is generated in the mind.

Purpose of this book

As part of my research into the brain I have discovered a really simple way to explain intelligence.

The purpose of this compact little book is to convey this approach to those who are intrigued by intelligence but not up for a long, heavy read.

This book uses simple everyday language and situations to explain how the brain gets us to build thoughts, use them to solve problems and start to innovate. It also explains how dreams are formed both during sleeping and daydreaming, and the important role emotions play in making us intelligent.

For those interested in building intelligence into computer games, simulations or physical robots, this approach is ideal as it requires no prior knowledge of artificial intelligence (AI).

Although the explanations in this book are extremely simple, the power of this approach lies in the fact that it is scalable. It can easily be translated into mathematical terms and programmed into robots and virtual characters.

To show how easily this can be done, I have added a robot control program 'flow chart' in *Appendix A – How to build machines with intelligence.*

It is simpler than you think!

You might well be surprised at how simple this approach turns out to be.

And you might think – why haven't others thought of this simple explanation of intelligence before.

My honest opinion is that they have been making things too complicated.

If we look around us at the time of this book going to press, we see that neurologists, psychologists and philosophers have widely varying definitions of what intelligence is and no single agreed view of how intelligence is generated in the mind.

This has prevented us from building machines with human-like intelligence, problem-solving skills and innovation.

In fact, many believe even the basics of how the brain works is still eluding experts in the field. This is evident from a recent quote from the journal Scope (published by Stanford Medicine): "The greatest challenge in the field of neuroscience, according to two experts, is that we still don't understand the basics."

This is the reason why we still do not see machines around us that are capable of the same kind of thinking, dreaming and problem-solving that humans do. But that is about to change…as I hope you will find out from this book.

What will you learn in this book?

Many of the points I raise will be explained using analogies from everyday situations.

By the end of this book, you will know how intelligence is basically generated in the brain and how we as humans start to think and solve problems.

This includes an explanation of why some people are more intelligent than others and why animals are not capable of human-like thinking.

This approach offers a clear explanation of how dreams are created in the brain when we sleep, or when we daydream, and explains the close relationship between dreaming and thinking.

This will set us on a path of understanding how our own intelligence works and how we can build human-like thinking and problem-solving skills into machines.

A SHORT STORY ABOUT A BOOKSHOP OWNER

My explanation of how the brain creates intelligence begins with a simple story about a bookshop owner. Her name is Lady Roseworthy and her bookshop is called Rosy's Books.

Lady Roseworthy wanted to get a little smarter about how she interacted with her customers. She wanted to find a better way of proposing new titles to customers based on their preferences. People came into her shop every day and told her, 'I like this author!' or 'I like crime thrillers!' or 'I like spy novels!'.

Lady Roseworthy would then have to apply her mind to try and think of similar titles she could suggest and which her customers might enjoy.

One day she got an idea and called her son Joe who was in his second year at university studying computer science. She told him of her plan to write down a long list of books with columns providing more detail about each book. Joe immediately suggested she rather use a software application than a document to make updating easier. He said that this will be much easier and the next Saturday he visited the shop and helped his mom record all the book titles into a long

Microsoft Excel spreadsheet. Like she had suggested, he added some columns to provide more descriptive information about each book. The following columns were added to the list:

- Title
- Author
- Genre
- Type e.g. paperback, hardcover
- Price
- Cupboard (the bookshop has 10 cupboards numbered from 1 to 10)
- Shelf (each cupboard has 5 shelves numbered from top to bottom)

'Good! Now I also know where to find them in the shop!' she complemented her son. 'But how do I sort them so that all the newest, best-selling books with the highest ratings are at the top? These are the ones I would like to recommend.'

'Simple,' Joe smiled. 'All we do is add three more columns with ratings for how new the book is, how many copies you have sold and what people have thought of it.'

'How will the ratings work?'

Joe thought about this for a moment.

'I think I have an idea!'

He grabbed a notepad and a pen and made some notes. Then he nodded and started explaining his approach to her.

To address the question of how popular a book is, he will add a column to insert the 5-star rating the book had received online from readers and reviewers i.e. a number between 1 and 5.

To address the question of how new a book is, he will add a rating out of 5 using a simple logic: 1 month old = 5; 2 months old = 4; 3 months old = 3, 4 months old = 2; more than 4 months old = 1.

To address the question as to how many copies had been

sold, he will write a little extra program to obtain this information from the bookshop's accounting software and then use the following simple logic to get a rating out of 5: 100 or less copies sold = 1; more than 100 but less than 200 copies sold = 2, more than 200 but less than 300 copies sold = 3, more than 300 but less than 400 copies sold = 4, 400 or more copies sold = 5.

'There you go! There are your three columns, Mom!' he said after adding it to the spreadsheet. 'Now I am going to make things even easier for you…'

'How?' she asked curiously.

'By multiplying these three ratings we can get a total rating…let's call it and Impact Factor…out of 125. This gives you a single number to judge the book on!'

'Oh!' she chuckled. 'His mother's good looks and his father's brains!'

'Let's see if it works…', he said. 'I have added 4 columns now…number of copies sold, popularity rating, how recent and this new Impact Factor!'

Joe pointed to a random book in the spreadsheet – *Sandelbury Summer* by Emelia Lothian.

The book had not attracted many positive responses online and was neither a new release nor a great seller. He checked the ratings:

1.) 2 stars for popularity or *impact*
2.) 1 star for number of copies sold or *repeats*
3.) 1 star for how new or *recency*

He then pointed at the last column containing the Impact Factor – the overall rating out of 125.
2 x 1 x 1 = 2 (that is 2 out of 125)

'That's very low – not a book you want to recommend to your customers,' he said. 'Let's choose another book – a newer release, something a little more popular…'

He selected a new book that had just arrived the previous month and was proving immensely popular with his mom's customers – *Zantanian Neolith* by Rodrigues Penansky. The book had attracted many positive responses online and Lady Roseworthy was hardly able to keep up with ordering more copies as they kept flying off the shelves. Joe checked the ratings:

1.) 5 stars for popularity or *impact*
2.) 5 stars for number of copies sold or *repeats*
3.) 4 stars for how new or *recency*

The Impact Factor was much better.
5 x 5 x 4 = 100 (that is 100 out of 125)

'That's pretty good! 100 out of 125! That's a book you can recommend!'

'This is so clever!' his mom smiled. 'I simply have to check this Impact Factor…this single rating out of 125!'

'Exactly. It does not need to take you a lot of time. You just filter the list for an author, or genre and the books with the highest Impact Factor will be at the top…those are the ones you can recommend…'

Rosy's Books Smart Search

Enter Author's Name or Genre

Dan Viandi

Find similar titles using

Impact Factor

Book Title	Genre	Impact Factor	
Death Valley	Suspense	122	Add to basket
Moose Mountain	Suspense	118	Add to basket
Coward's Cliff	Suspense	106	Add to basket
Dark Ravine	Crime	85	Add to basket
Angler's Pass	Suspense	83	Add to basket
Midnight Mayhem	Cult	79	Add to basket
The Lost Lake	Suspense	64	Add to basket
Dan Clarke's Journey	Autobiography	55	Add to basket

More

Figure 1. BOOK SEARCH BY AUTHOR NAME USING IMPACT FACTOR

Joe suggested they put two computers in the shop for customers with instructions on how to do searches using the Impact Factors.

The customers loved it!

(In Figure 1 we can see one of the first searches that was performed).

And the customers were talking about another feature Joe had added to the spreadsheet and which was causing a stir.

It was a random search mode – a bit like a wild card search that flashed up a new book title on the screen every three seconds. It basically just browsed through the newer and more popular books taking free reign. Joe called it 'Threading mode' and added a button which said 'Threading Mode' to the search box.

'How does this work, young man?' an elderly gentleman, who had already bought two books using Impact Factor searches, asked Joe.

'It's really simple,' Joe replied. 'It just uses the words in the title and start checking which of those words appear in some form in another book title. And it flashes up that title.'

'Is that all there is to it?'

'Well, it is a bit smarter than that – to start off with it looks for matches but also prioritizes titles with a high Impact Factor. If the Threading continues for a long time, it will eventually end up showing the books with lower Impact Factors.'

'Great! I am going to give it a try!'

'Oh, one more thing,' Joe said. 'When you feel the suggested titles drift too far from your original search title, you can just hit the Threading Mode button again and the program will restart Threading around your original title.' They ran the Threading mode using the man's suggested book title of *Death Valley* by Dan Viandi. They deliberately restarted the search after three suggested book titles. The screen is shown in Figure 2 below.

Rosy's Books Smart Search

Enter Search Title

Death Valley

Find "wildcard" titles starting with this book using

Threading Mode

	Book Title	Link Word	Impact Factor	
Start Here	**Death Valley**	Death	122	Add to basket
	Death Trap	Trap	119	Add to basket
	Speed Trap	Speed	107	Add to basket
	High Speed	-	86	Add to basket
Restart	**Death Valley**	Valley	122	Add to basket
	Valley Farm	Farm	101	Add to basket
	Organic Farming	Organic	94	Add to basket
	Organic Cooking	Cooking	74	Add to basket

Figure 2. WILDCARD SEARCH USING LINK WORDS AND THREADING MODE

We will soon see how helpful this short story about the bookshop is going to be when it comes to understanding the brain. That will allow us to quickly progress towards a principal understanding of how intelligence works in the brain.

Before we proceed though, please take another look at Figure 2 and how the link word 'Farm' from the title 'Valley Farm' was used to arrive at the next suggested title 'Organic Farming' whilst also considering the strength of the Impact Factor. As part of the process, the program also checked that the title has not been suggested before.

How is a bookshop important to understanding intelligence?

If we start to move our focus to the brain now, we can see the importance of the three aspects of *impact*, *repeats* and *recency*.

These are helpful in describing the impact a book has made on the public, but it is equally helpful to understand the impact a memory has made on the brain.

What do we mean by that?

To explain this aspect, we are going to look in a place not many researchers have looked for clues before. We are going to look at the phenomenon of dreaming. Yes, dreaming! Don't worry – it will soon make sense!

We can dream can we not?

When something happens to you, you will form a memory of that event. For instance, let's say on your tenth birthday your mom baked you a beautiful chocolate cake – the wonderful taste and all the fuss made for an intense 'emotional' experience and left a big impact on you. This ensured that this memory was prominently stored in your brain.

Another memory that was stored quite prominently in your brain was the image of the new football you had been playing with all week – as it had been in your thoughts all the time while you played with it.

Just before going to bed, you saw the cat run over the piano making a terrible noise just as everyone was going to bed. You quickly grabbed the cat and closed the piano to restore calm to the house.

With that, you jumped into bed and quickly dosed off.

The next morning you woke up and made your way to the kitchen where your mom was already preparing breakfast for everyone.

You immediately told her about what you had dreamt. Your dream revolved all around the birthday cake, the new football and the cat running over the piano. Of course, because it was a dream, it was somewhat contorted with a fair bit of drama thrown in, but the important question was:

What made you dream about those three items?

Those three memories were evoked by the brain, above all the other memories, because the experiences that caused them were either *emotionally intense (impact),* often *repeated* or very *recent*.

All three of these aspects will influence how strongly memories are stored in the brain – giving it the equivalent of an Impact Factor. When we say 'strongly', we mean how easy it will be for the brain to re-evoke or recall these memories in future.

If we think of memories as the impressions made by a car tire in the sand we can imagine rain water will fill it much easier if the tracks were deep from the start (*impact*), deepened by repetitive rolls (*repeated*) or just very fresh (*recent*) so that the wind did not have time to cover it with sand again.

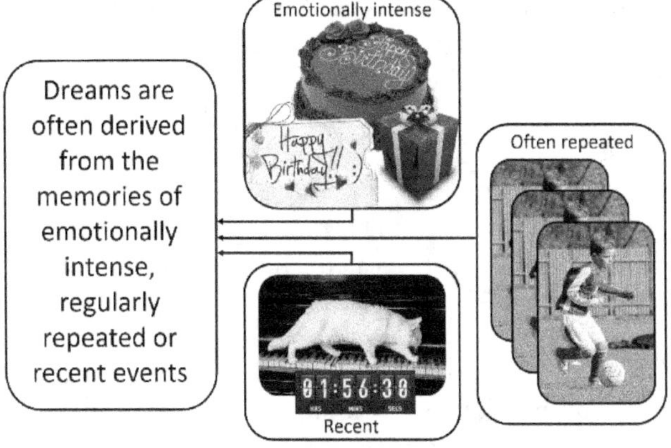

Figure 3. THE TYPES OF MEMORIES FAVOURED BY DREAMS

When the rain starts falling, the water will tend to follow the deepest ruts as water always follows the way of least resistance. In a way the signals that flow in the brain do the same thing and will automatically flow in the 'deepest ruts' formed by emotional intensity or *impact*, *repetition* and *recency*. The strongest memories will therefore be re-evoked first – those with the highest Impact Factor.

Sometimes we try to hide things from ourselves or deem them to be unimportant in our lives, but when they come up in our dreams, we realize that we might have undervalued their emotional importance.

After some contemplation, it is often apparent why the brain chose a certain metaphor to represent a deep-rooted fear we might be hiding from ourselves and others.

Dreaming about this metaphor object is driven by its link to the underlying fear and will reemphasize this fear's emotional importance (*impact*) to the brain and also increase its Impact Factor (since it has also now been *repeated* and is more *recent*).

This will make it more likely that this fear (and its causes) will come up in our minds the next day when we are awake and encourage us to act on it. Unmasking hidden fears or issues like this might serve some primordial survival function and could be one of the reasons why we dream.

We quickly learn that, when we study for an exam, we must repeat the facts over and over again, use colored pens and vivid diagrams and we must not study too long before the actual exam else we will forget all the facts. This is all to make sure we can easily recall the memorized study material when required to do so in the exam.

In this book we will be talking a lot about the mechanism of dreaming. Please do not let that put you off. Just because others have not defined dreaming in the manner I have, and not used it in their explanation of intelligence, does not mean we cannot do so.

Remember my promise to you that at the end of this book, you will understand the basics of how intelligence works in the brain!

Daydreaming

We have spoken about sleep dreaming. Now let's talk about daydreaming.

Do you sometimes sit at a coffee shop and as you sip your coffee your thoughts just start to drift away?

When the brain is relaxed and does not have an immediate problem to solve, it will start to daydream. We can say this is equivalent to Threading.

Just like Joe's program jumped from book to book using some shared link word, our brains will start linking memories using some shared aspect (similar to a link word).

One after the other our brains will present these memories to us in the form of recalled visual images, whilst also re-evoking the emotions associated with these images.

Because our brains have no problem to solve during daydreaming, it will not drive us to do anything. We might still 'recognize' significant objects in our environment, but these will just restart the Threading process around what we have noticed and not make us do anything.

For instance, we might spot a lady with a friendly dog at a table in the coffee shop and the sight of the dog will remind us of a Missing Dog poster we had seen on a number of lamp posts a few weeks ago.

The image of the poster will come up in our minds and we will feel the strong emotions we had felt every time we saw the photo of the little missing dog.

Next our brains might use the concept of the dog (just like the link word) and Thread to our neighbor who had just the previous day invited us over to show off his new dog.

It was an exciting event and as we recall the images of the neighbor egging on his little puppy to do tricks, we feel again the happy emotions that we were experiencing at the time.

The daydreaming process is nothing other than our minds going into Threading mode and flashing up visual images (with their emotions) one after the other – and these will tend to be centered around things that have happened to us that had made a strong *emotional impression* (good or bad), things that were *repeated* often or events that have happened *recently*. If we notice an interesting new object while daydreaming, the Threading process might be restarted around this object.

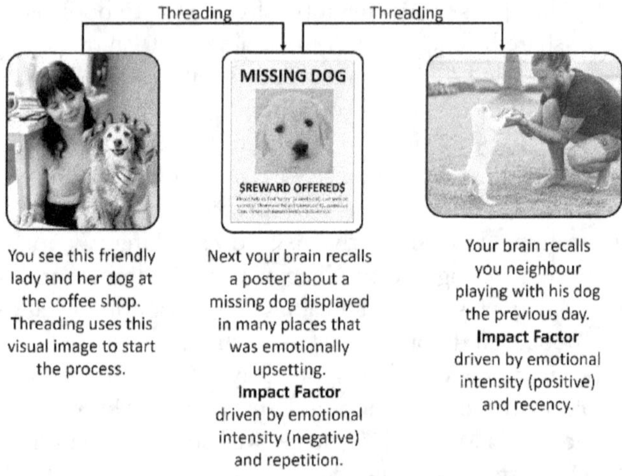

Figure 4. THREADING MAKES US DAYDREAM

Any new motion within our field of view will attract our attention. This observed motion could spur a miniscule amount of adrenaline release, causing a slight tension which refocuses the Threading process. This tension will be relieved once we have identified the moving object as harmless. This could be part of a primitive survival instinct.

Chatting - how did we get onto this topic?

Let's say your friend Nina now joins you at the coffee shop and you just start a casual conversation with her that carries on for a few minutes.

After a while you ask Nina:

'How did we get to talk about…microplastics?'

And Nina starts tracing back how the conversation had

started and flowed to that point, saying: 'Well, you said your dad works at the university, and then we spoke about the riots at the university, and then you said your sister attended the riots and is such a rebel and that's why she likes to wear a bright red hat and red lipstick and then I started talking about the microplastics in lipstick…'

'Oh, yes – now I remember!'

Why did the conversation evolve like this?

This is a good example of a casual discussion where no questions or problems had to be resolved urgently and it was just a good old chat.

Both minds are just in 'wondering' or Threading mode and two people will let their brains bring up whatever they choose and share these topics with one another including the emotional aspects which often form the gist of the discussion e.g. was it good or bad, right or wrong, fair or unfair, etc. The aim is usually to entertain, strengthen relationships, garner some sympathy – and perhaps enjoy a little humor.

Now let's take a closer look at how these two wondering minds Threaded through the train of thoughts.

The discussion started with you mentioning your dad's job at the university.

Nina then mentioned the riots at the university.

This happened because in her mind the concept 'university' was closely linked to the recent violent riots at the university.

This association involved a strong emotional impact because students were injured during the protests. It has also been repeated often in newscasts of which the latest one Nina listened to in her car on the way to the coffee shop. It therefore had a high Impact Factor in her mind.

In your own mind you also saw the TV coverage of the riots, but you were shocked when you saw a young woman with a red hat and red lipstick as you knew it could have been your sister.

This evoked anger in you because you thought your

sister was being overly rebellious just to get attention. One of her annoying traits (in your opinion) is the bright red lipstick that she always wears.

By you mentioning her red lipstick, Nina's mind jumped to an article she was writing for her blog on microplastics in lipstick. This was upfront in her mind as she needed to get it posted before the end of the day to meet the deadline.

In this way their minds jumped from memory to memory by linking key aspects in what the one said with what was related and prominent in the other person's mind.

It is the similarity in this aspect (link word) that forms the connection to the other person's association, and because there is no urgent need to address a problem, this casual conversation in effect becomes a joint Threading or daydreaming exercise.

Both brains were allowed to 'freewheel' and put on the table anything it could come up with that might be of interest…and both Nina and you enjoyed this interaction because it provided an opportunity to share thoughts and talk about the emotional effect these things were having on your lives. (This process is depicted in Figure 5).

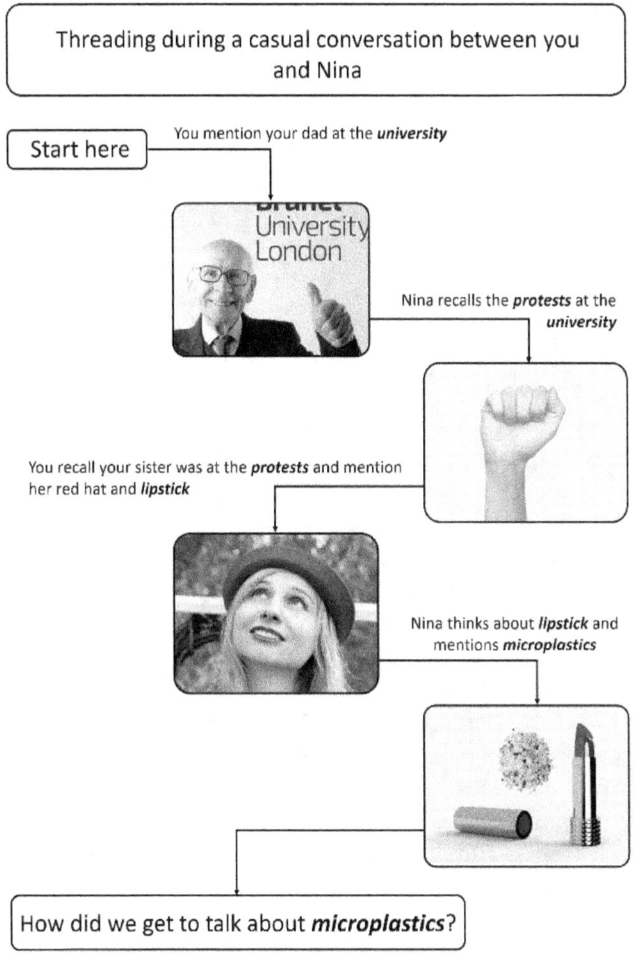

Figure 5. THREADING DURING A CASUAL CONVERSATION

THINKING – SOLVING A PROBLEM

We are still at the coffeeshop. But now something has happened. Your casual chat with Nina has gone into a 'problem solving' type discussion.

Nina suddenly looks worried.

'I have bought this lovely new jacket but they taped it up inside this box so heavily, I can't open it.'

'Let's take a look,' you say. 'Yes, I see it does look like it is going to be tough to open.'

'Do you perhaps have a sharp object with you?' Nina asks. 'Something like a pair of scissors? Or can we get a knife from the kitchen?'

'Hmmm, let me think…what can we use…'

Both you and Nina inspect the box with the thick layers of tape again.

'A car key?'

'I have tried that on the way here,' Nina says. 'The tape is too thick.'

'I am just thinking,' you say to Nina. 'If one could find something like a nail clipper…?'

Nina runs her fingers over the packaging tape again.

'I know!' she suddenly says and start rummaging through her bag. 'I'll try this old ballpoint pen.'

After a few pokes with the ballpoint pen, she suddenly manages to break through the tape and start opening the box.

'Bingo! I got it! What do you think of my jacket?'

She holds up her new jacket.

'That is a truly gorgeous jacket! I love it!' you say. 'That calls for two more lattés!'

Again, we should look carefully at this joint effort and see how we can relate this situation to what happened at the bookshop. We saw how the casual conversation between yourself and Nina was maintained by a joint Threading process. But when Nina started struggling to open the cardboard box, both brains went into 'problem-solving' mode.

When the brain goes into 'problem-solving' mode it cannot afford to just let thoughts be generated randomly as happens during Threading.

The thoughts now need to become relevant and helpful to solving the problem.

To stop the brain from allowing thoughts to just drift off randomly, the person must now encourage the brain to think about the problem and only come up with memories that can help solve the problem.

Our brains learn during early development that it can limit the diversion into random thoughts by refocusing the brain on a problem.

Sounds familiar?

Yes, this is exactly what Joe's program did when he had it in Threading mode and then hit the Threading Mode button again – to restart and refocus the process. This brought the search back to the original book title.

From a young age we learn we can direct this constant Threading of memories that takes place in our brains so that it will bring up helpful ideas around the problem we are trying to solve and not 'wonder' off onto irrelevant topics.

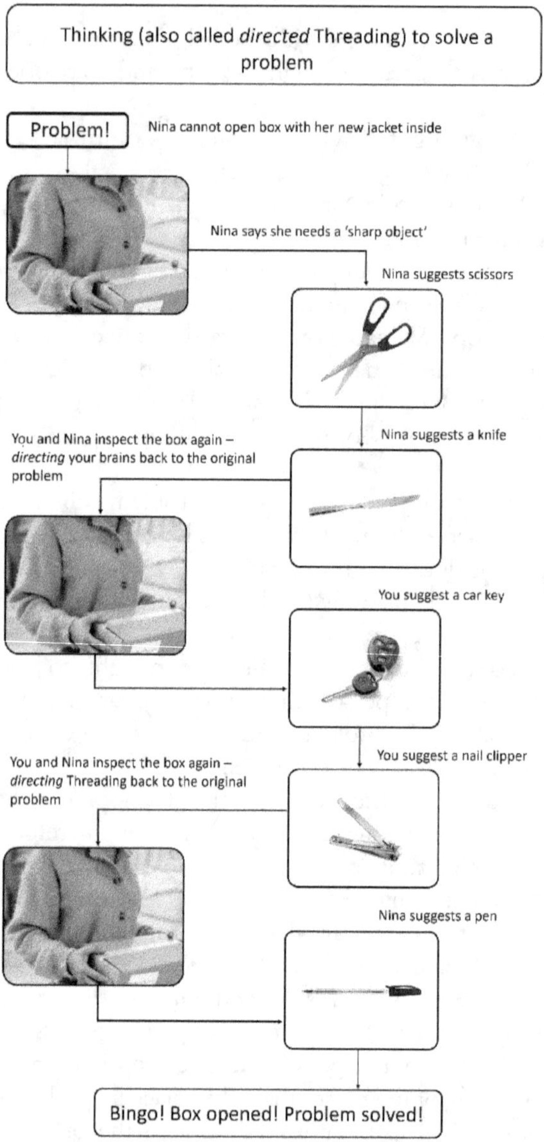

Figure 6. *DIRECTED* THREADING TO SOLVE A PROBLEM

When we watch someone who is trying to direct the Threading in his or her mind towards solving a specific problem, we might observe some interesting behaviors, including:

- Staring at the problem area for a long time.
- Touching or holding it in different ways.
- Viewing it from different angles.
- Closing eyes to avoid distractions from others and the environment.
- Ask other people to keep quiet so they can 'think'.
- Repeating phrases like: 'Let's see! What can we do about this?
- Saying: 'What did I do last time?'
- Seeking advice from others.
- Drawing sketches or diagrams on a piece of paper to capture the essence of the problem.
- Searching the Internet for advice and ideas.

This will help the brain avoid straying from the topic and encourage it to recall memories around the problem that might be helpful in finding a solution.

Threading is a continuous process in the mind and is either *undirected* (e.g. casual conversations, daydreaming, sleeping, etc.) or *directed* (e.g. thinking, problem solving, innovation, creating, etc.).

We will define Thinking as nothing other than *directed* Threading.

By the way, we capitalize terms like Threading and Thinking to indicate that we are referring to the definitions used in this book.

We *direct* the Threading by focusing on the problem and by avoiding distractions from the environment. By doing this we hope we can use the actions from a previous stored experience to solve a current problem. Sometimes our brains will provide an immediately relevant memory to us – and we will be 'confident' about our solution. On other occasions there may not be such a clear match between the problem we are faced with and the memories we are presented with by the brain – and we will be less confident about having found a solution.

What makes us think?

Everything starts with our emotions. Emotions drive behavior. Intelligence does not drive behavior, but informs and refines behavior.

In my guide *Understanding Emotions: For designers of humanoid robots* I explain how all our motivations start with regulating mechanisms deep in the brain called Urgency To Restore mechanisms. The brain cleverly rents some real-estate in the somatosensory (body map) area of the brain and represents the status of these Urgency To Restore functions as if these were 'senses' – meaning the brain constantly stays aware of them as they are visceral (body) feelings.

These feelings are our emotions and they teach us to steer away from certain situations (avoidance states) and drive us towards other situations (pursual states). Avoidance states are what we learn to call 'bad' and pursual states we call 'good'.

We learn through reinforcement learning how to act on our emotions in what becomes a lifelong pursuit of good feelings (happiness) and avoidance of bad feelings (unhappiness).

Based on my approach in *Understanding Emotions: For designers of humanoid robots* we can define emotions in mathematical terms. It is easy now to assign a value to a good emotion (between 0% and +100%) and a bad emotion (between 0% and -100%). This will be part of the Impact Factor of an association. The *emotional intensity* at the time of saving an association will be similar to the *impact* or popularity rating used to calculate the Impact Factor for the books in Lady Roseworthy's bookshop.

Now let's look at an example where your brain starts to Think!

Imagine you are feeling hungry. The problem your brain now needs to solve is to find a food source. Your hunger pangs effectively send a message to the brain and it will start to search for memories around food sources. This is similar to entering the search word 'Hungry' into an Internet browser and it will bring up webpages about 'hunger' and 'food sources'.

The brain will recall associations around food. We might recall a juicy hamburger we had eaten the day before, or a piece of cheesecake we enjoyed with our coffee.

The associations that will come up first will be the *emotionally intense*, *recent* or the ones that have been *repeated* often. You might almost immediately think of your favorite hotdog that you love and order almost every week.

As these associations around food sources are evoked by the brain, so are the learned actions we should perform to obtain these food sources. These actions could include walking to the refrigerator to fetch a salad. Or it can be a sequence of actions like getting your wallet, picking up your car keys, starting the car and driving to the drive thru.

Remember, the emotion of hunger (because we deem this to be an emotion) drives the behavior by fetching the prescribed actions from memory for execution.

The brain will strongly bias us towards the best tasting food (most *intense*) but perhaps modify our response based on considerations like…how expensive the food is…how far we have to walk…or perhaps how healthy the food is. And so the brain will provide us with the actions we need to perform to navigate to the food source.

This is a clear instance where the brain has used Thinking to solve a problem.

Similarly, when we have to solve a trigonometry problem during a school exam, we will Think about the problem presented to us. In this case our brains will again go into solve mode and try to present us with information about how similar problems were solved in the past. It will present helpful principles and patterns that we have learned when we studied for the exam. The quicker we can use these principals and patterns to solve the trigonometry problems, the higher our score will be and the more intelligent others will think we are.

The role of adrenaline in Thinking is also interesting. We often get that queasy feeling on our stomachs before an exam. This fear of failing releases adrenaline into our bodies and helps us focus on the exam. The emotions that drive us to perform well in the exam are not directly related to our physical bodily needs like hunger or thirst, but could be driven by the fear of not getting grades to go to university or the fear of disappointing our parents.

In the end, it is simply our emotions that drive the Thinking process. That is why we always say: emotions can exist without intelligence, but intelligence cannot exist without emotions.

Emotions tell us what we must do, whilst intelligence (Thinking) tells us how we must do it.

Context

One often hears artificial intelligence experts say that the challenge with building truly humanoid robots is the fact that robots can still not understand 'context'.

With the approach described in this book, it is easy to understand how our brains (and the brains of robots) can constantly obtain the context of what is being thought about or being observed.

This is because these incoming 'observed' mental states are constantly being compared to what is already in the brain (compared with the association database).

If what is being thought about or observed cannot be matched with what is in the brain, the brain will evoke the closest association along with its emotions.

Let's say you are watching TV and see a whale swim between some icebergs. Although you have not seen this specific whale before, you have seen other whales like this one. The whales in your mind might be from a whale watching cruise in Norway, where an Australian climate change activist had delivered an impassioned speech about global warming and sea level rise. You signed up to their organization and offered to do a webinar on 'Designing a Low-carbon Smart City' but you were now becoming concerned about media reports about failing smart city projects around the world.

All of the above facts will be brought up in your mind because of Threading.

We haven't mentioned this before, but Threading can be an extremely fast process in the brain. Threading will link all of the above separate (but linked) concepts together in a fraction of a second – so that the brain runs through all of what was experienced, along with the emotions generated, and then hold on to the strongest associations or one that is of emotional value (e.g. fear of not being able to make a low-carbon case for a smart city).

In an instant the image of the whale had linked all you know and deem important about whales in your life, as well as the wider context around sustainability and climate change, in your brain.

This is how the brain manages to unlock the contexts around a thought or observation – almost instantaneously.

Because Threading like this will quickly re-evoke different emotions, we provide robots and virtual agents with facial expressions based on averaged emotions. This prevents jittery smiles and frowns, and a smoother natural-looking expression. Just like human facial expressions, only the averaged emotion is displayed.

SO WHAT IS INTELLIGENCE?

Intelligence is all about finding solutions to problems using *directed* Threading. We have chosen to call this Thinking.

We say somebody is highly intelligent if they can quickly find a good solution to a problem using Thinking or *directed* Threading. And we say somebody is not intelligent when they struggle to quickly come up with a good solution. A few things will need to happen in the brain to make it intelligent:

1.) It must store memories (learn) and include the *emotional impact* (good or bad), *recency* and *repetition* as part of the association (these make up the Impact Factor)
2.) It must be able to Thread efficiently.
3.) It must be able to perform effective Thinking i.e. *directed* Threading.

If the brain can perform the above three functions, it will save memories effectively, retrieve linked memories effectively and direct the brain towards helpful memories effectively.

This will enable it to solve new problems effectively.

Try this personal experiment to get a feel for how this mechanism works in your own brain:

Let your mind drift off into a bit of a daydream and then identify some of the thoughts that it came up with. Test these by checking if they were important in your life in terms of *emotional impact* (good or bad), if they were *recent* or if they were regularly *repeated*.

Now present yourself with a simple problem e.g. imagine you must go outside and put a plant you have bought in a pot. Follow your mind as it thinks about the new plant, about the garden shed where you keep the potting soil, then see how the visual images of your previous potting experience come up in your mind and the tools you used. You might even recall snippets from the YouTube channel about pot plants you visited at the time.

This is the brain at work! And you should be able to see first-hand how your brain uses *directed* Threading to offer you ideas from your past to help you solve your current problem.

Congratulations, if all of this went well – you can assume yourself to be an intelligent person!

Are you an artist or an engineer?

Everyone is different. No two brains are the same.

Some people's brains will naturally search more narrowly around a problem area – taking a detailed view when performing *directed* Threading. Others might naturally do a wider search when seeking solutions. These are functions of the biology of the brain (inherited genetics) and not really something one has control over.

One can of course learn techniques to improve your ability to effectively perform *directed* Threading.

People learn to use simple rules, diagrams, books, proven methodologies, prescribed approaches, procedures and advice from experts to help them direct their brains. And of course, in today's world, we keep links to Internet sites where we have previously found helpful advice.

Sometimes when engineers are fixated on solving a problem, someone might say: 'We must think outside the box! We are thinking too narrowly!' On another occasion someone might complain that artists are scatterbrains and allow too much loose ideas (Threading) to influence their judgement.

I often get accused of both: 'You are the biggest nerd!' or 'You are such a dreamer!'

People who naturally concentrate their minds on detail might be good at mathematics, science, analytical tasks, research, etc. While those who tend to think 'wider' might be better at intuitive tasks, the arts, life sciences, motivational speaking, strategy setting, etc.

This is where the power of diversity comes in. It is easy to get stuck in one perspective when the optimal solution might be hiding in another. For this reason, boards and advisory panels are often composed of members from a wide variety of backgrounds and disciplines.

I have found, while building intelligence into simulated characters and robots using this approach, I was able to program their brains to Think more like artists or more like engineers.

This can be achieved by simply adjusting the level of 'correlation' required between link words and associations.

For an artist a memory typified by the link word 'car' can Thread to an association of a 'horse cart' or 'golf cart' – thus quite wide.

While for an engineer it can for instance only Thread to 'motorcar' or 'racing car' – thus much narrower.

There is also the potential to modify the brains of robots to perform both types of Thinking at the same time. Or we can use more than one robot – all with different Threading techniques. This can create a powerful swarm of 'problem-solving' robots presenting a wide range of diverse views!

The importance of emotions

It is not always easy to see where emotions fit into all of this. Psychologists and neurobiologists tell us that emotions are important in learning and problem-solving, but not exactly how this works in the brain.

From the simple approach presented in this book we can immediately see where emotions fit in.

Firstly, emotions drive all behaviors via Urgency To Restore functions (like get food, get water, avoid pain, avoid fear, get oxygen, avoid exertion, etc.). The status of these 'utility functions', as they are also called, is represented as 'sensory states' (body feelings) which teaches us to do things to act on these emotions to keep them in balance.

Secondly, the above emotions are stored as part of every association we make. Emotions can therefore be re-evoked from objects in our memory to which they have become attached. It is the *intensity* part of the Impact Factor of an association – and can be good or bad.

In the case of a new association or memory being created we see that the association gets stored more vividly when a strong emotion is present at the time of forming.

As emotions are activated either from the Urgency To Restore functions or from recalled memories – the brain will only act on the strongest emotion from either these two sources and this will drive our behavior.

Again, to find out exactly how emotions work in the brain, and how they can be easily integrated with the explanation of intelligence in this book, I want to refer you to my guide *Understanding Emotions: For designers of humanoid robots*. It is a short book in the same vain as this one.

These two compact books on intelligence and emotions provide explanations that handshake perfectly and form two key building blocks of a brain model I have developed called the Xzistor Concept brain model. This model allows us to design and build robots and virtual agents with intelligence and emotions.

To keep the explanation of intelligence simple in this book we will assume we can indicate a negative emotion as a percentage between 0% and -100%, and as a positive emotion as a percentage between 0% and +100%.

Is the Internet our second brains?

It is interesting to see just how similar an Internet browser is to the way our brains work.

We have all these stored webpages, and when we enter a search word or phrase, the browser will find the websites which contain the search word we have entered.

But the algorithms performing these searches also factor in the popularity of websites (*impact*), how many visitors they have received (*repetition*) and how current (*recent*) the websites are.

This is nothing other than a type of Impact Factor.

We can now present the Internet browser with our question or search topic, which is effectively the 'problem' – and it will look for stored information (memories) that could provide an answer or 'solution' to the problem.

Just like the brain, the solution offered might not provide a precise answer but more of a suggestion for our consideration. We can still decide if we want to use the information or not.

If the websites presented by the search are not really relevant or helpful, and we cannot use the information to solve our problems, we can always refine our search by being more specific in our choice of search terms.

Just like we learn to *direct* Threading to find helpful information stored in our brains, we learn to direct Internet searches to find helpful information stored on the Internet. And just like those who prove good at retrieving helpful information from their brains are deemed 'clever', those able to retrieve useful answers from the Internet, will also be deemed 'clever'.

In today's world it is quite possible for a person not regarded as very intelligent by others, to solve problems better than most by making effective use of the Internet.

Many people have become very reliant on solving problems using the Internet and might find themselves in a muddle if they should lose access to the Internet.

The Internet really has become like a second brain to many – including myself.

Language

Language development can easily be explained by this approach as it naturally results from Thinking and learning. Just like we learn to repeat muscular hand movements to open a bag of sweets, we can learn to instead use words to solve the problem: 'I want sweets!'

All that changed was that instead of using the muscles of the hands and arms to open the bag of sweets, we learn that squeezing air through our vocal cords, and articulating words using mouth and throat muscles, can achieve the same (of course if there is someone around that cares enough about us!).

I have a very interesting ongoing research project where I am teaching a small robot to talk.

Using the above principle, we teach the robot to not navigate to the food source, but to 'ask' for food instead. Once the robot has learnt that this works, it will prefer to 'ask' for food in future as these robots are made to constantly consider 'economy of effort' i.e. they are inherently 'lazy'.

What is so fascinating about this approach is that we can rapidly expand the robot's vocabulary by the tutor providing the robot with emotional reward (praise) for learning new words – just like we see parents do with their children.

You will find more information about this project on the Xzistor LAB website under the Blue Sky Lab area.

CAN INTELLIGENCE BE IMPROVED?

It is not easy to manipulate the way our brains store memories. But luckily there are many ways that those not gifted with a lightning fast and effective way to *direct* Threading, can get better at it. A lot has got to do with how you stop your brain from Threading off into irrelevant areas and help it to stick with the search topic.

Whilst at school and battling with my homework my mom often had to tell me:

'Stop thinking about other things, and concentrate on your homework!'

What she was actually saying was: Stop Threading and activate *directed* Threading.

There are many books on how to improve your concentration and mental alertness. Getting enough sleep and exercise, as well as eating a healthy diet, will help keep the brain alert.

There are also techniques one can use to 'encourage' your brain to retrieve helpful memories. The principal idea is to flood the brain with information particular to the problem and force it to focus on the detail that could link it to past experiences (memories) that will cast light on how to solve a current problem.

To further develop this skill one can make use of a set of spoken or unspoken questions that you ask yourself when trying to solve a problem. This will help focus the brain.

How about another mind experiment?

Let's assume you are in a light aircraft full of passengers and the pilot loses consciousness. You have never flown a small aircraft before. You now have a problem – you must quickly figure out how to control the aircraft. Under severe pressure you might start asking yourself some questions out loud:

'How do I control this thing?'

'Is that the steering wheel?'

You get into the pilot seat.

'Right! Where is the throttle – I need to maintain forward speed!'

'Altitude – I must maintain altitude!'

Scenes from movies where a character was subjected to a similar situation might now start to flash up in your mind.

'Radio! I must contact the tower! Get some directions from the air traffic controllers!'

'Where's the radio? Can I talk into this thing? Wait – push the button first!'

'Hello, ground control. This is Cessna Mike Zulu Yankee – we have an emergency!'

Of course, under the circumstances, the adrenaline in your body will help you to focus on the situation – in fact that is exactly what adrenaline is for.

By asking the right questions you can help direct your brain to quickly bring up relevant information that might help you control the aircraft.

Let's assume it all ended well – you received good instructions from the tower and managed to land the aircraft safely.

Phew!

The questions you ask when addressing new problems need not be spoken out loud and can be inaudible thoughts used to focus the mind.

Fixing your bicycle's gears on the garage floor might involve a few unspoken questions like:

'Where should I do this?'

'I don't want to get grease all over the place. I need to put some old newspapers down first…'

'What tools do I need for this job?'

'Where are the bicycle tools?'

'In the shed – I need to find the key for the shed?'

'Where did I last see the key for the shed?'

These questions become part of a standard set of cues directing the brain to find solutions in a logical fashion.

If the brain immediately finds the correct answer, solving the problem will not be a trial and error effort. It happens so quickly that it becomes a smooth process comprising a coordinated set of activities.

We see that robots using this approach start off with jolty motions and then, as they keep on learning, end up with faster, smoother movements.

You will have full confidence in your chosen actions when fixing your gears if you know you have performed these many times before, and you will not experience any tension or uncertainty as to whether your approach will solve the problem or not – no adrenaline needed in this case!

My brain went into automatic mode

Have you ever driven home after work and when you got home you realized you never even thought about driving – you just suddenly found yourself at home.

This happened because you were following learned behaviors that you have repeated many times before and did not have to 'solve a problem'.

A situation like this will require minimal Thinking, perhaps just while overtaking one or two cars and avoiding a new pothole in the road, but it should really be a stress-free journey.

On trips like this, our brains can afford to just Thread and either we end up just thinking about stuff (daydreaming) or perhaps listening to the radio.

But if on the way home you suddenly come across new roadworks and you are diverted into a part of the city that you have never been in before – you now need to snap out of your Threading (daydreaming) mode and start focusing.

The fear of getting lost (we deem this an emotion) has now become a problem again and the brain needs to *direct* the Threading towards the unfamiliar road signs and try and find clues on navigating home from an unknown location.

Yip – that niggly feeling in the pit of your stomach is adrenaline. This is what snaps you out of Threading mode and helps you to fade away any irrelevant thoughts.

So, in the one instance, almost no Thinking is required with lots of daydreaming, and in the other case intense concentration (i.e. *directed* Threading) is required to get you home.

(I just realized 'concentration' is a good word to describe this focusing of the brain – this *directing* of Threading around a specific topic).

INNOVATION AND CREATIVITY

What is innovation?

Innovation simply refers to new solutions delivered by Thinking.

It is interesting to note that our ability to Think (i.e. effectively control the Threading process) very much effects our progression through life and often determines what social and economic standing we achieve. It is almost universally accepted that a high intelligence is a good thing which leads to good outcomes in the lives of people and their communities.

But it is not always that simple.

When we look at intelligence in relation to innovation, we see that the more developed or 'intelligent' nations of the world, in spite of constantly delivering many technologically advanced solutions, still struggle with the common evils of economic instability, political turmoil, corruption, inequality, pollution, criminality, substance abuse, international conflicts, etc.

One can therefore not say intelligence is per se a good thing. It depends on what it is used for. And those societies and individuals on the high end of the intelligence and innovation scale, will only unleash the full power of innovation when it is not driven by short-term materialistic gain and exclusive enrichment, but by a holistic worldview of orderly co-existence, equality and sustainability.

What is creativity?

Sometimes the problem we are trying to solve only consists of a vague idea or notion of some improvement that can benefit ourselves or others.

We might for instance have a desire to create an innovative new solution that will enrich lives by offering a tangible solution like an engineering design or perhaps an emotional, intellectual, artistic or entertainment-orientated solution.

The value of the creation could lie in its ability to solve a technical problem or it could just be something that provides entertainment or is aesthetically pleasing. Often it is a combination of more than one of these aspects.

Our brains learn that satisfaction can be gained from creating such completely new objects or artefacts, whether it be a stylish piece of furniture, a modern architectural building or even just…a new explanation of intelligence.

For a new high-performance sports car, it could involve both designing the power plant and drive train, and the outer body which people will need to find visually appealing.

Some brains can conjure up a novel solution to a new problem in minutes – and through effective Thinking find from abstract aspects in existing memories the inspiration to come up with something completely original. Some brains get 'educated' to have this ability and some are naturally born with this creative streak.

Normally, a new creation will start with undirected Threading to assess different alternatives, then move to *directed* Threading where Thinking will be used to refine the detail around the creation and perfect the solution.

Abstract art

Even when the brain does not recognize what it is looking at, it cannot stop searching for associations that bears some correlation with what is being observed.

The brain can never stop Threading and therefore never stop recalling associations and emotions (remember that every association has a 'net' emotion attached to it that gets re-evoked when the association is recalled).

So even if an artist has simply dropped a few quick brush strokes onto a canvas, and this contorted arrangement does not portray any object known to man, the brain will still insist on presenting the viewer with some emotions based on the artwork. We might hear someone say: 'I cannot really see what she painted here…but this bit reminds me of a dead tree…and this looks like the face of a man in pain…it's like a war zone…'

What the abstract artist achieves is conjuring up a single emotion that represents the net of a complex mix of emotions that would hardly be generated in normal everyday life.

This enables the artist to create an unusual and unique emotional state within the observer's mind by forcing the brain to combine image elements and emotions to end up with an interesting resultant 'feeling'.

As the viewer explores different areas of the painting, the net emotion might change based on the specific objects portrayed in the painting. And in this way abstract art can create complex new emotions based on Threading and what one can call 'deliberately unrealistic compositions'.

DO ANIMALS THINK?

One of the interesting realizations I came to while developing the Xzistor Concept brain model was that animals do not Think – at least not like humans do.

I know this might be difficult for many to accept, but allow me to explain.

Animals do Threading because we see them dream when they sleep. Often you will see the paws of a dog twitch rhythmically as if the dog is running and chasing something. The dog might also make some muffled barking noises. These are just signs that the drugs in the brain which are supposed to switch off the messages to the muscles during sleep are not 100% effective.

So, if animals can Thread…why can't they Think?

When an animal solves a problem, it is mostly by instinct or reinforcement learning (if you have not already done so please read up on the interesting experiments Ivan Pavlov did while researching the brains of dogs).

This means we can teach a dog to do things to get food, but it will not learn to effectively *direct* its Threading to come up with new ideas. The dog will struggle to use the actions of a stored memory to try and solve a current problem.

Animal intelligence is therefore something different

from human intelligence – animals cannot Think and they cannot innovate in the manner we have defined it.

We sometimes see birds use stems of grass to lift ants from holes in tree trunks, but this use of tools does not originate from Thinking.

If animals were able to Think, their behaviors would have been typified by a rapid progression towards the type of innovation and problem-solving we see in humans, including a sense of 'awareness' or 'self' and a sense of own mortality. They would also have developed language – both spoken and written.

We don't see this in animals.

This limits the 'understanding' of animals in terms of real-life context and it becomes difficult to guess what is going through a dog's mind when it is lying on the porch watching the street.

This is also why animals do not get bored…because they do not get emotional reward from solving problems and being innovative. Yes, they can get stressed if forced to lie around too long without physical exercise, but they need this by instinct. This is different from the *intellectual* manner in which humans get bored.

Just to be clear, this does not mean that animals do not have emotions. It is all too evident that dogs have emotions when we stroke them.

Remember what we said: There can be emotion without intelligence, but not intelligence without emotion (of course I am referring to human-like intelligence as described in this book).

I sometimes think it is a good thing that only one species on Earth was gifted with Thinking and the ability to innovate, else things could have been a lot more eventful on an already busy planet!

CAN MACHINES THINK?

Intelligence as part of a wider understanding of the brain

Of course, the detail around everything we have discussed up to now can be vastly expanded, but the aim of this book was to provide you with a simple understanding of intelligence.

I have already mentioned that I have developed a complete cognitive model of the brain.

This Xzistor Concept brain model not only explains how emotions and intelligence work in the brain, but also many other aspects like sensing, reflexes, learning, navigation, pain, fear, phobia, aggression, love, language, curiosity, depression, addiction, intuition, etc. (You can find out more about my brain model here: **www.xzistor.com**).

When one develops a brain model like this you inevitably reaches a point where you begin to wonder what will happen if you build this logic into a device like a simple robot – will it become lifelike and display actual intelligence?

This sent me down a path where I ended up having a lot fun building simulated and physical robots that use this type of Thinking or *directed* Threading to solve problems.

All that was required was for the robot or simulated character to store associations and keep track of their *emotional impact* (good or bad), *recency* and *repetition*. This can be combined into an Impact Factor which is attached to each association.

By giving the robot certain 'utility functions' or mission objectives, I could let it act on the related emotions and use *directed* Threading to search for memories containing learned behaviors that could help solve problems – exactly as it happens in the human brain.

Because these robots were able to Thread, they were effectively able to daydream and sleep dream as well.

I designed them so that I could switch them to sleep mode by pressing a key on the keyboard. This cut all sensory stimuli and impeded all motor movements. The brain then just kept on Threading (the basis of sleep dreaming) since there are no sensory stimuli to steer or *direct* the Threading.

Daydreaming works fundamentally the same but now we allow sensory stimuli to restart the Threading process.

If the robot is in daydreaming mode it does not have a reason to move around and the sensory inputs will therefore not change much.

The robot will however recognize a visual image placed in front of its video camera and restart the Threading process around this image. I will not go into any more detail here, but if you want to use this approach to build intelligence into virtual agents and robots, please see *Appendix A – How to build machines with intelligence.*

For those of you who are just curious, I have made a demo video about hunger as experienced by Xzistor robots which I think you might find interesting.

You will find it on my YouTube channel here:
https://youtu.be/aEHGuQhTRiE

Figure 7. SIMULATED ROBOT IN A LEARNING CONFINE

Figure 8. PHYSICAL ROBOT WITH INTELLIGENCE AND EMOTIONS

A final word on intelligence

I really hope you have found our discussion on intelligence interesting. All of this has been a fascinating journey for me spanning more than 20 years. Please do not stop your exploration of the brain here, and remember you can always follow my research at the Xzistor LAB (my home neuro-robotics laboratory). Just go to my website here: **www.xzistor.com**. I also provide some guidance on the website as to how you can set up your own home AI lab and program robots using the principles you have learnt here: **https://www.xzistor.com/build-your-own-ai-lab/**

Just to summarize one final time:

Our brains Thread all the time. This allows us to dream during sleep and also to daydream.

Sleep dreaming does not interfere with the Threading process, while during daydreaming we might 'recognize' objects in the environment which could restart or refocus the Threading process.

Recognizing something simply means finding a match for that object (i.e. its sensory state) in our minds and doing some quick Threading around the topic to obtain the relevant emotions and contexts of the object.

We learn to use *directed* Threading to help us solve problems and we call this Thinking.

The faster and more effectively someone's Thinking is – the more intelligent we say that person is.

Emotions play a key role in intelligence. Emotions make us do things to restore or rebalance 'utility functions'. The emotion routine also uses the *emotional intensity* part of the Impact Factor to help estimate which association will most likely provide the best actions to resolve an unbalanced emotion.

It is also the satisfaction (or fixing) of an unbalanced emotion that signals to the brain to store the performed behaviors for future use (i.e. reinforcement learning).

In this way we keep on learning and expanding our

association database for solving problems in future.

All of what was said in this book can be translated into mathematics – providing us with mathematical definitions for intelligence that can be programmed into robots.

My Xzistor Concept brain model, of which intelligence is just one part, allows us now to program virtual agents and robots to have human-like intelligence and emotions.

These are certainly interesting times.

Our understanding of the brain has moved to a mathematical model that we can run on computers. This can help explain many of its hidden mysteries and elusive mechanisms, and assist in improving many medical and psychological conditions.

We can also now build machines that think more like humans and begin to understand 'context'. Although this process will take time, we are slowly starting to catch up with science fiction and stepping through an inevitable door into the future. We are entering an era where the brain is starting to understand itself – a milestone that will only come around once in the evolutionary journey of mankind…

APPENDIX A – HOW TO BUILD MACHINES WITH INTELLIGENCE

Introduction

I have used the explanation of intelligence in this book to build intelligence into both simulated and physical robots and I it worked really well – this is because intelligence can be written in mathematical terms and programmed into digital and neural network devices.

My many late nights were rewarded when I saw how these virtual and physical robots came to life and started to act in a very human-like manner.

I called this my Pinocchio moment!

After initial testing and proving the concept using my 'Simmy' simulation (see Figure A.1 below), I embarked on designing and building a physical robot called 'Troopy' in a similar 'learning confine'. Troopy was based on the Lego Mindstorms EV3 platform but using the leJOS firmware replacement so that I could program it in Java.

It worked great!

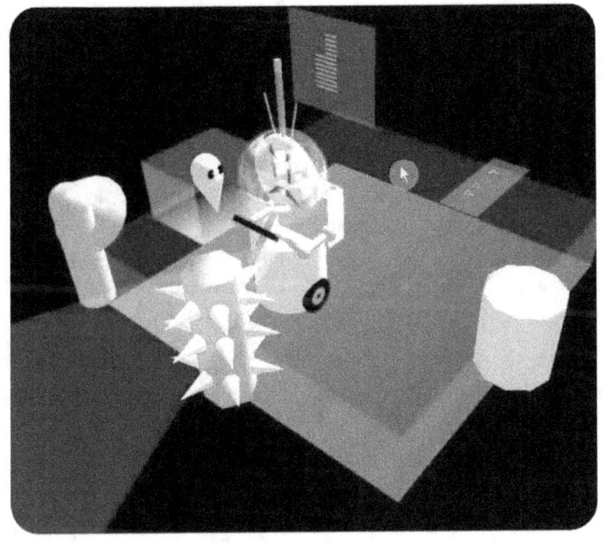

Figure A.1. VIRTUAL ROBOT'S PAINFUL ENCOUNTER WITH CACTUS

In Figure A.2 below we can see Troopy being taught by myself – driven from the keyboard – to navigate to the 'food source' and push Button No 1 on its Head Up Display (HUD) panel to access the food (Troopy does not really eat food – it only feels that way!).

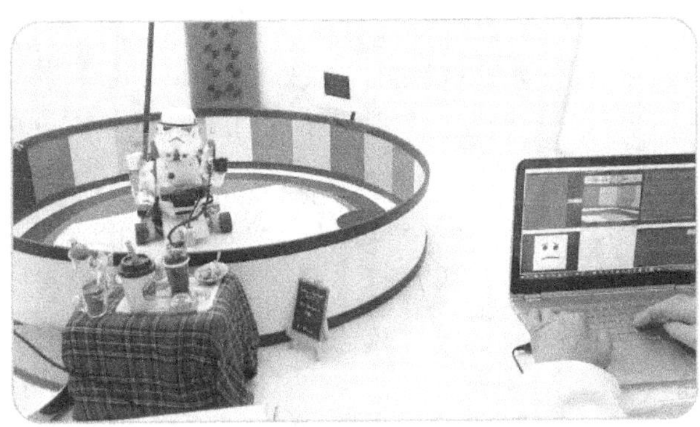

Figure A.2. PHYSICAL ROBOT TAUGHT TO FIND FOOD

In Figure A.2 we can see a few interesting aspects around Troopy. We see it is a differential drive robot with a left and right wheel motor. Troopy can move its right hand up and down to push 4 buttons on its translucent panel (not so clear in this image). Using the HD video camera (dark object on torso) to navigate its way, Troopy uses the color sensors (one front and one rear pointing down at color patterns on the floor) to know when it has reached the food source. This works like a tactile (touch) sense.

For this basic test Troopy's visual sensing is limited to recognizing color panels around the wall of the learning confine. Each color panel is given a unique number. This tells Troopy where he is in the confine.

Towards the right I can be seen 'teaching' Troopy by sending motion commands via Wi-Fi. A dashboard flashes up on the computer screen when the robot control program is running, providing real-time graphs showing the 'critical' parameters and emotions as they are being generated. It also includes what the robot is seeing on video and a simple facial expression pane for a quick-look view of Troopy's average emotional state.

Robot control program (flow chart)

In the flow chart depicted in Figure A.3 below I have provided the logical building blocks of how this approach can be implemented into a computer program controlling a robot.

I will describe each block shown in the flow chart in more detail, but before doing so, it might be helpful to first clarify a few aspects around this diagram.

A powerful aspect of the Xzistor Concept architecture is that it allows a robot to perform all the general functions the designer wants it to perform, whilst at the same time developing emotions and intelligence.

For instance, you could have a robot with general duties

to retrieve unexploded incendiary devices from an active battlefield and bring them to a facility where these can be safely dismantled. The explosive devices can be brought into a dedicated zone within the facility and placed in one of five 'dismantling areas' based on size, weight and visual assessment (e.g. using conventional AI).

Since the situation on the battlefield can constantly change, this is where we want the robot to autonomously Think about problems and solve these based on what it has learnt in the past.

Once the robot reaches the demolition facility with the unexploded items, it simply follows clearly demarcated routes within the building and deposits the items into one of the dismantling bins. The general duty functions the robot performs inside the facility do not require autonomous Thinking or problem-solving as these do not change (this is not to say the robot cannot use conventional artificial intelligence or machine learning techniques to support routine functions) .

It is on the battlefield where the situational scenario and terrain can suddenly change, and objects and obstructions can be introduced indicating either a new friendly activity or a new enemy threat. This is where we want the robot to learn to Think autonomously and make decisions about new situations based on past experience.

We will define a REFLEX BLOCK where we let the robot perform all its general duty functions – we will refer to these as routine functions. Like the reflexes performed by humans, this area requires no inputs from the Thinking and intelligence part of the robot control program.

While the program is performing these routine functions, the robot will however keep a close eye on its 'utility functions'.

What do we mean with 'utility functions'?

These are health and housekeeping functions that are aimed at keeping the robot safe and operational. An example of a utility function is maintaining the robot's battery level of charge at an appropriate level. When the level of charge drops below a critical value, the robot will know that it is becoming urgent to restore the battery charge level. But because the locations of the charging stations can change, we want the robot to do some learning around recognizing and navigating to the nearest charging station (keeping in mind that the nearest charging station might be on a mobile support vehicle).

We need the robot to become intelligent.

In the Xzistor Concept brain model 'utility functions' form the basis of emotions. When utility functions go out of balance and need to be restored – this will trigger a negative emotion (0% to -100%) which the robot will feel as a sensory state. And when the utility function is being restored – this will trigger a positive emotion (0% to +100%) which the robot will also feel and learn from. As part of the robot's learning, these emotion values will be included in associations (via Impact Factors) that are formed and stored in the robot's association database.

These emotions in the database can be re-evoked when associations are recalled (meaning the robot will feel them again as sensory body states).

The robot can for example recognize an object that it had viewed when a utility function was being restored (perhaps the view of a battery charging station) and this will re-evoke the positive emotion experienced at the time. In the eyes of the robot the charging station will become a 'good thing' that is not a 'threat'.

Objects will start to have positive or negative emotions attached to them. This will help the robot understand whether these objects should be pursued (good) or avoided (bad) on the battlefield. For its own survival it will become highly judgmental on an object to object basis.

The human mind does not work much different.

Whether an emotion is generated directly from the status of a 'utility function', or from being part of an association which is being re-evoked, doesn't really matter to us. We just want to know if we should act on an emotion or not i.e. if it is strong enough.

If a specific emotion is strong enough, and we need the robot to do something about it, we will let the robot use Thinking to try and find a solution to the problem. It will forget about the routine functions for a while and try to restore the upset emotion using past learning based on what is being observed (sensed) in the environment.

All that is required from the control program is to 'filter' the association database using 1.) the emotion ID (e.g. hunger = 101) and 2.) the sensory states (e.g. video images) defining the robot's current location and orientation in its environment. The retrieved associations and stored actions would have been formed in exactly that position and orientation, and would have addressed that same emotion. This ensures only relevant actions are suggested to solve the emotion.

This identification process can happen so fast and learned action commands retrieved so quickly, that the robot will seem to move smoothly and confidently from any point in the confine to the food source.

A simple example of the above is where we give a robot in a learning confine a utility function of pain.

If the robot crashes into the wall of the learning confine, it will feel pain.

Next time the robot gets to the same area of the learning confine it will 'recognize' that it is coming close to the wall where it had felt pain, and feel the negative emotion being re-evoked. This will feel like pain, but without the tactile (touch) part. This strong re-evoked emotion can only be remedied by the robot moving away from the wall. When the robot does this, it will feel a positive emotion akin to 'relief'.

When we as humans experience these emotions, we sometimes refer to them as 'fears'. We might say something like: 'I avoid running into walls, out of 'fear' of getting hurt…'

The robot learns to avoid colliding with walls based on the fear emotion it experiences.

This prevents the robot from being damaged.

We see the robot carry on with its routine functions until it visually recognizes that it is moving too close to a wall, upon which it will experience fear (re-evoked negative emotion based on a painful experience) and quickly direct itself away from the wall before carrying on with its routine functions again.

Just like humans, these Xzistor robots are driven by emotions whilst intelligence (Thinking) provides useful information around what actions to take.

Robots really become lifelike when they act like this!

The final part of the flow chart is where the actions (e.g. wheel motions) are executed based on what was provided by the Thinking routine.

The robot finds these actions (wheel motor speeds) in the association database. The robot might go something like this:

I have a strong 'battery low' emotion. I need to act on this. I am seeing a charging station dead ahead of me. Last time I felt this emotion and saw a similar charging station, I just moved forward with left and right wheel speeds of +60rpm and it worked. I will try these wheel speeds again now.

As the robot docks with the charging station, the battery level of charge utility function will see a rise – and in doing so the emotion will go from negative to positive and the actions performed will be reinforced and stored in the association database for future use.

Simple isn't it? But remember Xzistor robots can be scaled up to almost infinite complexity – especially if we use neural networks to achieve all of the above. And suddenly you will have a robot that experiences and acts on emotions and intelligence just like humans do!

We will now discuss each block in the diagram in more detail (please refer to Figure A.3).

1. START ROBOT

This is where we start the robot up. This action will include all power-up, initialization, built-in tests, confirming communications like Wi-Fi, Bluetooth, microwave, radio, satellite communications, etc. It might include confirming GPS tracking is active.

In the case of Troopy, our little Lego robot, this involved switching on power to the robot via an umbilical (with slipring), starting up the Java Virtual Machine on the single board computer on the robot, connecting the Wi-Fi and Bluetooth links between the robot and the computer, activating the HD video camera on the robot and confirming the video signal is received by the computer via umbilical (including USB).

Then we compile and run the robot control program on the computer (Java with leJOS plugin within an Eclipse environment).

A dashboard with many graphs will flash up on the computer screen and the video image of what the robot sees will also appear on the screen. The operator can now steer the robot and control its motors from the keyboard to teach the robot.

2. REFLEX BLOCK

This is where the robot control program (brain) enters the main loop and allow the robot to perform its routine functions. In this area we can program the robot to perform any tasks we want it to do. None of these routine functions will require Thinking or innovation as described in this book.

It is a handy area to just let the robot do stuff and we don't really care as it doesn't really interact with the intelligence algorithms of the program.

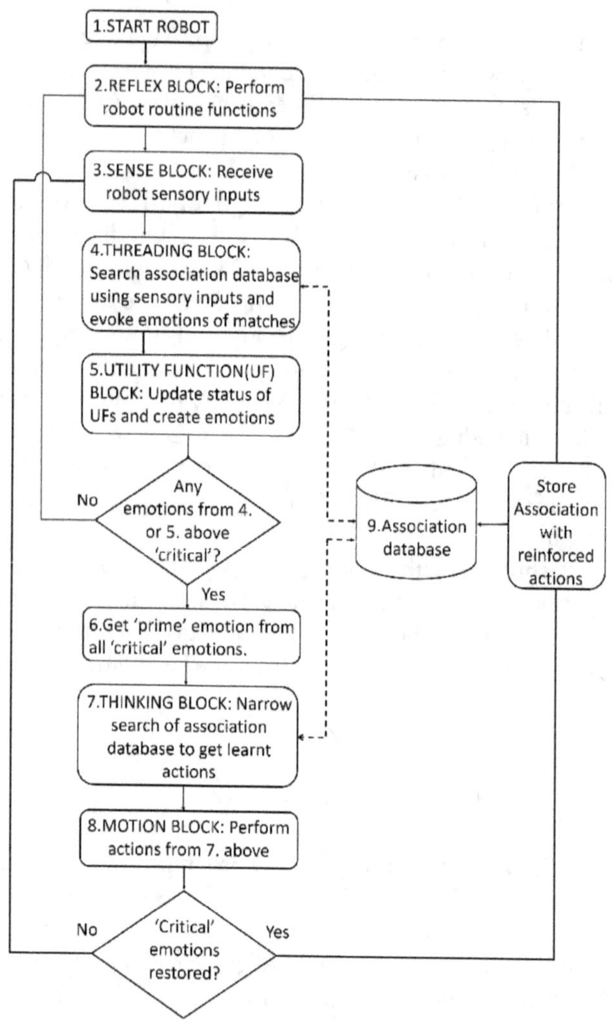

Figure A.3. ROBOT CONTROL PROGRAM (FLOW CHART)

This does not mean we can't use conventional artificial intelligence or machine learning techniques here or not make use of the robot's sensors for these routine functions – but the information we store in this area will be separate from the robot's association database (memory). In terms of the Xzistor Concept brain architecture these routine functions are just reflex behaviors. No utility functions or emotions required for 'intelligence' are processed in this area.

3.   SENSE BLOCK

This is where we receive the sensor inputs used to provide the robot with senses. This tells the robot about its environment and can include visual sensing (video), tactile (touch), temperature, sound, olfactory, humidity, inertia, acceleration, balance, etc. These sensory states will be saved along with associations and used to 'recognize' these states in future. If a sensory state experienced by the robot correlates closely enough with one in the association database (memory), this sensed state can be 'recognized' and the association will be recalled or re-evoked.

4.   THREADING BLOCK

Here the robot brain will perform Threading and constantly bring up stored associations (along with stored emotions). As the robot observes its environment via its senses, these sensory states will be used to search its association database and could result in 'recognitions' (see broken line in Figure A.3).

If the sensory inputs being experienced correlate with those which were stored as an association, the association will be unlocked and re-evoked – including the emotional part. This means the robot will remember what was stored and feel that same emotion again.

If the sensory inputs being experienced do not correlate well with those which were stored in the association database, the 'closest match' association will be unlocked and re-evoked – including the emotional part. This means the robot will feel the emotion of a closely matched experience.

If a robot needs to solve a new problem within the environment, the Threading will tend to become *directed* (i.e. towards Thinking).

Where the robot's activities are very familiar and require no focus or problem-solving, the Threading will tend to be undirected (i.e. towards daydreaming).

This block will constantly generate emotions by re-evoking associations.

If these emotions from recalling associations are stronger than those generated by 'utility functions', they will start to drive behavior – either pursual or avoidance.

5.   UTILITY FUNCTION BLOCK

The utility functions are responsible for forming the original emotions.

As we have said before, when utility functions go out of balance and need to be restored – this will trigger a negative emotion (0% to -100%) in the robot.

And when the utility function is being restored – this will trigger a positive emotion (0% to +100%) in the robot.

The robot will become aware of utility functions when they go 'critical' – meaning they have exceeded some predetermined threshold value and now need attention.

This block will constantly generate emotions from utility functions and compare these with the emotions generated from associations (recalling).

The program will select the highest of these – called the 'prime' emotion – and focus on finding actions and behaviors that would restore it to normal.

Humans do the same thing when they feel they need to attend to a number of different things at once – they will attend to the most urgent first.

QUESTION: Any emotions from 4. Or 5. above 'critical'? If No, return to 2. REFLEX BLOCK and continue executing routine functions while also constantly going through the loop to check on utility functions and emotions. If Yes, proceed to step 6. and obtain the 'prime' emotion from all the 'critical' emotions.

Restoring this 'prime' emotion is now the problem the robot needs to solve using Thinking.

7. THINKING BLOCK

This is where we narrow the search of the association database to get relevant 'learnt' actions. The program will focus on that part of the database used to store associations related to the 'prime' emotion. For this 'prime' emotion it will extract associations that shows a high correlation with that physical location and orientation in the environment – this means the robot will use information about the environment to 'recognize' and unlock the most appropriate association in the database.

Sensing a new trench on a battlefield might let the robot bring up associations about how to reverse and circumvent such a hazard, whilst sensing an enemy actor might bring up associations explaining how to move to a position of cover.

In both these cases, the 'prime' emotion might be fear and the robot might have been trained to understand falling into a ditch or into enemy hands will cause pain.

When Troopy goes into Thinking mode we simply allow it a few milliseconds to find an accurate association match, after which we force it to 'try' the actions of the closest matching associations.

We make Troopy 'beep' every time it needs to activate Thinking mode.

When Troopy has received a lot of training to solve problems there is not a lot of beeping. But early on, when the little robot has only been shown a new task a few times, there is a lot of beeping and jolty movements in an attempt to autonomously solve the problem.

After a while, if Troopy cannot solve the problem (e.g. navigate towards the food source) and the 'prime' emotion (hunger) becomes too strong, Troopy will start to 'cry' to indicate that help is needed from the tutor.

In the end it was not Troopy's impressive ability to autonomously generate 'intelligence' that made this little robot so likable – but its moments of vulnerability and desperation…

8.   MOTION BLOCK

Here we perform the actions suggested by the Thinking routine in 7. THINKING BLOCK. (The 2. REFLEX BLOCK will separately send motion commands to the motors and effectors in aid of the routine functions).

For a simple robot like Troopy in a learning confine, these could be limited to wheel motor speeds, LED light patterns, speaker sounds and also hand motions (just up and down) to push buttons on a Head Up Display panel.

QUESTION: Has the 'prime' emotion been restored?
If No, return to 3. SENSING BLOCK.
If Yes, store (or update) successful actions along with all sensory information to the association database and return to 2. REFLEX BLOCK.

What happens at this point in the program is that, now that the robot has tried the actions obtained from the association database using Thinking, it simply goes back to see if the actions taken had changed anything.

Before carrying on Thinking about this problem, the program will check if changes had taken place that could perhaps be restoring the upset emotion, or perhaps now another emotion had gained enough strength to become the 'prime' emotion needing attention.

Only after these facts have been established will the program return to Thinking about the current 'prime' emotion and try to resolve it.

9.   ASSOCIATION BLOCK

This is the area where we will save associations to the association database. We will also direct the program to this block if we want to search for an association – either for undirected Threading purposes (daydreaming) or to perform *directed* Threading (Thinking) to solve a problem (see broken lines in Figure A.3).

The association database is a simple 2-dimensional array as shown in Figure A.4. Each association will comprise one row of comma separated values representing brain states as explained in Figure A.5.

The number of rows will grow as the robot moves about and associations are formed based on sensory state changes.

The advantage of using a learning confine is that it has a finite number of sensory states – so a finite number of associations can be created (once these have been formed it is just a matter of updating them).

It is important that we do not move objects around too much in the learning confine and we should keep the lighting consistent.

Because Troopy gets grumpy (aggressive) when there is too much light in the learning confine, the little robot had me perplexed with its moodiness and uncooperative stance until I realized the blinds in my laboratory were letting in too much sunlight. Troopy is programmed to experience an aggressive emotion when it sees the color white, so if there is too much natural light, some of the color panels in his learning confine start to look white to it.

If you want to see Troopy get angry, here is a demo video: **https://youtu.be/qFsyNgs7xGM**

The robot should store associations as fast as things happen. Depending on the experiences of the robot, these associations will include positive and/or negative emotions. For learning we are specifically interested in associations that form when a problem is being solved.

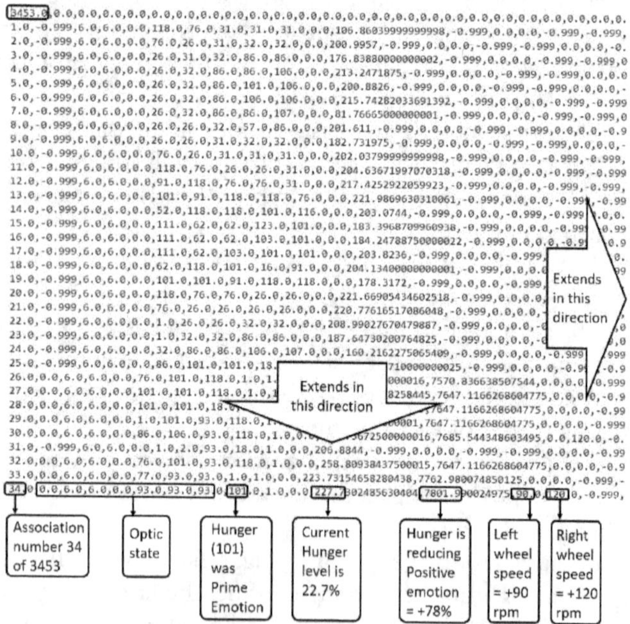

Figure A.4. ABSTRACT FROM AN ACTUAL ASSOCIATION DATABASE

These will contain a strong positive emotion and point to the successful behaviors that solved the problem (reinforcement learning). These behaviors will be favored when next the problem must be solved. The strong positive emotion will give the association a high Impact Factor which increases its chances of being the preferred association to be recalled when solving this problem in future.

If you train Troopy to drink water, you will quickly see it starting to favor a milkshake based on the higher Impact Factor (tastes better – and solves emotions driven by both the thirst and nutrition 'utility functions').

In a changing indoors or outdoors environment the number of associations will grow quickly and require some innovative data processing approaches or neural network solutions because of the volume of data.

Figure A.4 shows an abstract from Troopy's actual association database. Figure A.5 shows the constituent parts of a simple association in more detail.

It is important to note that the 2-dimensional array shown in Figure A.4 actually extends in both width and length, but this abstract is adequate for our discussion. The last association in the list (number 34.0) was formed whilst Troopy was successfully moving towards a food source and pushing the correct button to access the food.

In future, if hunger becomes the 'prime' emotion again and Troopy is in exactly the same place, this association will be accessed and the wheel speeds (and directions) listed here will be repeated.

By pushing a single key on the computer keyboard while Troopy's control program is running, the whole association database can be exported as a .txt file. To avoid having to train Troopy all over when we switch it off, we can import this association database after starting the robot up again by pressing a single key on the keyboard and all that it has learnt will be back in its brain. In this way learning between robots can be shared or a collective association database can be used (in future perhaps cloud-based).

Like I have said before: If we can store memories effectively, Thread effectively and Think effectively – we can design machines that will have built-in intelligence and emotions that are principally no different from humans!

Typical association format

An association comprises a single row of comma separated values with e.g. 42 values:
1,2,3,4,5,6,7,8,9,10,11,12,13,14,15,16,17,18,19,20,21,22,23,24,25,26,27,28,
29,30,31,32,33,34,35,36,37,38,39,40,41,42

Position 1 – 5 : Unique identifier
Position 6: Emotion ID (based on utility function)
Position 7: Net emotion (+ or -)
Position 8: How recent
Position 9: How many times evoked and updated
Position 10: Impact Factor
Position 11: Front tactile sensor (pressure between 1 and 5)
Position 12: Rear tactile sensor (pressure between 1 and 5)
Position 13 – 33: Optic sensor (video frame reduced to 20 numbers)
Position 34: Emotion 1
Position 35: Utility function 1 positive emotion (+%)
Position 36: Utility function 1 negative emotion (-%)
Position 37: Emotion 2
Position 38: Utility function 2 positive emotion (+%)
Position 39: Utility function 2 negative emotion (-%)
Position 40: Left wheel speed (0 – 100 rpm)(- = reverse and + = forward)
Position 41: Right wheel speed (0 – 100 rpm)(- = reverse and + = forward)
Position 42: Hand motor speed (0 – 1000 rpm)(- = reverse and + = forward)

Figure A.5. TYPICAL ASSOCIATION FORMAT

I encourage you to try this approach to build real intelligence into your own robotic applications. I hope you will have fun and learn something!

Remember to read my guide *Understanding Emotions: For designers of humanoid robots* (Amazon) if you are looking for and equally straightforward explanation of emotions and a way to program them into robots in a way that integrates perfectly with the approach to intelligence in this book. Let us know how you get on and don't be shy to share your work!

ABOUT THE AUTHOR

Rocco Van Schalkwyk is a mechanical engineer with 30 years' experience in the aerospace, defense and nuclear industries. Having published a number of books, he taught himself C++ and Java and started developing virtual and physical robots running on his patented Xzistor Concept brain model – an integrated brain model that allows robots to experience emotions and intelligence based on human brain functionality.

You can find out more about his research on the **Xzistor LAB**'s website here:

www.xzistor.com

www.ingramcontent.com/pod-product-compliance
Lightning Source LLC
Chambersburg PA
CBHW061733250726
48657CB00002B/903